Water Bugs and Dragonflies

Water Bugs and Dragonflies

Explaining Death to Young Children

Written by
Doris Stickney

Illustrated by
Meredith Gould

United Church Press/The Pilgrim Press
700 Prospect Avenue East
Cleveland, Ohio 44115-1100
thepilgrimpress.com

Adapted from "Death" (*Colloquy*, volume 3, number 11, December 1970).

Printed on acid-free paper.

26 25 24 23 22   1 2 3 4 5

Library of Congress Cataloging-in-Publication Data on file
LCCN: 2021943793

ISBN 978-0-8298-1834-5

Printed in The United States of America.

Introduction

Looking for a meaningful way to explain the death of a five-year-old boy to his neighborhood friends, the pastor of the local church reflected on the transition of a water bug into a dragonfly—and Doris Stickney, the pastor's wife, adapted the story into a graceful fable that she published as part of her article, "Death," in the periodical *Colloquy* (December 1970).

But the tragic death of a young boy was not the only death Doris Stickney contemplated in her writing that year. Preceding "Death" in *Colloquy* was an article in the *United Church Herald* (May 1970), in which Stickney shared her own sobering news:

"You are an intelligent woman," the doctor said quietly. "So you will not think it is a death sentence when I tell you that your condition is what we call lymphatic leukemia.

It may be controlled, which means that you could live on for many years." I had known that there was cause for concern, but somehow the breath-catching word "leukemia" found me unprepared.

Stickney's reflection, "Benediction: The Living Part of Death," revealed the attitude she and her husband shared regarding honest conversations about death:

No evasion of the truth was called for, we decided. Always, in our growing family, we had tried to meet life's misfortunes calmly, without hysterics. We would expect to meet the uncertain future in the same spirit.

A statement of Unamuno became mine: "Sow the living part of yourselves in the furrows of life." I soon discovered that the battle was not won by splendid statements. Life would not leave me alone. It called for decisions. I renewed my concert subscription, ordered new stationery, and pledged help to program chairmen of groups to which I belong.

It's as simple as this: I can withdraw inside myself, pull down the shades and wait. Or I can open the curtains and see what the day promises.

For choosing to open the curtains with each new day, and for gifting the story of *Water Bugs and Dragonflies* to others even in the face of her own cancer diagnosis, we remain grateful to Doris Stickney.

Down below the surface of a quiet pond
lived a little colony of water bugs.

They were a happy colony, living far away from the sun. For many months, they were very busy, scurrying over the soft mud on the bottom of the pond.

They noticed that every once in a while one of their
colony seemed to lose interest in going about with
its friends. Clinging to the stem of a pond lily, it
gradually moved out of sight and was seen no more.

"Look!" said one of the water bugs to another.
"One of our colony is climbing up the lily stalk.
Where do you suppose she is going?" Up, up, up she
went slowly. Even as they watched, the water bug
disappeared from sight.

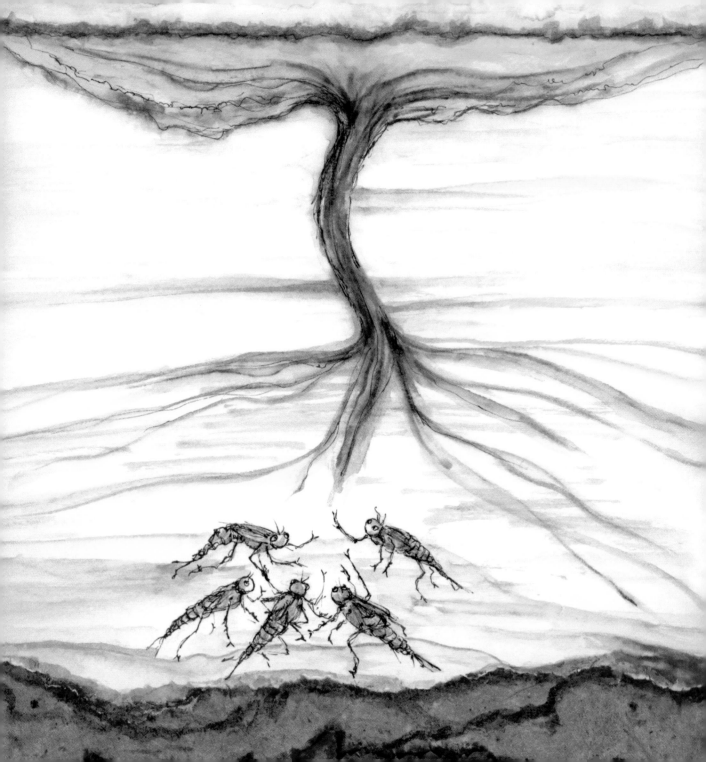

Her friends waited and waited but she didn't return. "That's funny!" said one water bug. "Wasn't she happy here?" asked a second water bug. "Where do you suppose she went?" wondered a third. No one had an answer. They were greatly puzzled.

Finally one of the water bugs, a leader in the colony, gathered the bugs together. "I have an idea. The next one of us who climbs up the lily stalk must promise to come back and tell us where they went and why." "We promise," they said solemnly.

One spring day, not long after, the very water bug who had suggested the plan found himself climbing up the lily stalk. Up, up, up he went.

Before he knew what was happening, he had broken
through the surface of the water and fallen onto the
broad, green lily pad above. Weary from his journey,
he slept.

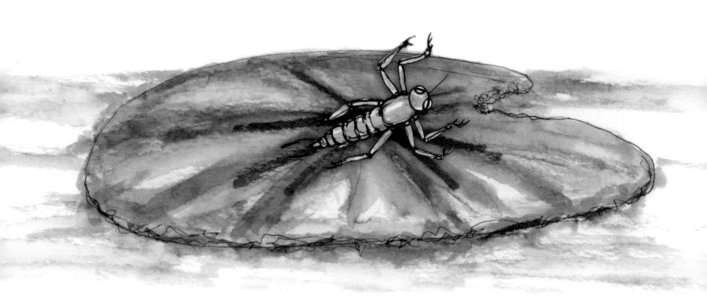

When he awoke, he looked about with surprise. He couldn't believe what he saw. A startling change had come to his old body. His movement revealed four silver wings and a long tail. Even as he struggled, he felt an impulse to move his wings. The warmth of the sun soon dried the moisture from the new body.

He moved his wings again and suddenly found himself up above the water. He had become a dragonfly. Swooping and dipping in great curves, he flew through the air. He felt exhilarated in the new atmosphere.

By and by, the new dragonfly lighted happily on a lily pad to rest. Then it was that he chanced to look below to the bottom of the pond.

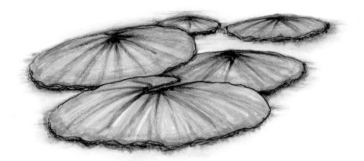

Why, he was right above his old friends, the water bugs! There they were, scurrying about, just as he had been doing some time before. Then the dragonfly remembered the promise: "The next one of us who climbs up the lily stalk will come back and tell where they went and why."

Without thinking, the dragonfly darted down. Suddenly he hit the surface of the water and bounced away. Now that he was a dragonfly, he could no longer go into the water.

"I can't return!" he said in dismay. "I tried, but I can't keep my promise. Even if I could go back, not one of the water bugs would know me in my new body."

"I guess I'll just have to wait until they become dragonflies too. Then they'll understand what happened to me and where I went."

And the dragonfly winged off happily in its wonderful new world of sun and air.

An Excerpt of "Death"

Doris Stickney

Your children's world is full of friends. Then suddenly one is taken by death. Almost every day to some parent or teacher comes the question, "Where has Bobby gone?"

Somehow, the answers of an earlier generation now have a hollow sound. Our parents replied: "He has gone to heaven" or "He has gone to be with God." Today's children live in a world of scientific excursions into the heavens. … The old answers will not satisfy today's children.

Nor is one ever prepared for tragedy. Such was the case in our little community. Our five-year-old son and his playmate, Bobby, were inseparable companions. Full of energy, they played games or took turns on a neighbor's swing. We loved to see them together.

One summer afternoon as Bobby was swinging, the crosspiece holding the ropes fell suddenly forward. It struck the little boy a crushing blow, taking his life in an instant.

We parents of the neighborhood were terribly shaken. Of course, death had entered our lives before. It was not a new experience for any one of us. But what should we say to our children in answer to the inevitable questions? We must find words that would not only satisfy them but our own adult minds as well.

It fell to my husband, as pastor of the church, to hold the service in memory of Bobby. In preparing what he should say, he recalled a boyhood experience:

"When I was only nine years old," he said to me, "our young minister told us boys the fable of the water bug who changed into a dragonfly. [T]he fact that I have remembered it all these years makes me think I should tell it at Bobby's service. It might be helpful to the parents and the children there."

So Doris Stickney's husband told the story of a water bug's transition to help parents and children in the wake of Bobby's death, and Doris in turn penned the fable to help children around the world make sense of death. She concluded in her article, "Death":

No one can ever predict the reaction of children to a story. The world of imagination is more real to them than the visible one. They surprise us with their clear grasp of that which we would make complex. And with unerring honesty, they see through our flimsy pretenses. "I don't know," is an honest admission. But "I believe" gives our children confidence in a future to be anticipated and in a Creator whose plan can be trusted.

Published in *Colloquy: Education in Church and Society* (December 1970).